Dark Buttercream
Vanilla buttercream

Cashew Brittle
*Hard toffee with cashews
and shredded coconut*

Butterscotch
*Firm brown
vanilla b*

Butterchew
*brown sugar
with milk
te coating*

Dark Walnut
English walnuts

Milk Almonds
Roasted almonds

Dark Almonds
Roasted almonds

P-Nut Crunch
*Crunchy peanut
butter center*

Milk Pattie
Vanilla caramel

Dark Pattie
*Vanilla caramel with
dark chocolate coating*

Ginger
Glacéd ginger

Scotchmallow
*Honey marshmallow
and caramel*

Light Chocolate Truffle
*Rich chocolate buttercream
with ground nutmeats
on top*

Mocha
*Coffee milk chocolate
buttercream*

Dark Nougat
*nougat, coconut,
la, with almonds*

Dark Chocolate Truffle
*Rich chocolate buttercream
with ground nutmeats
on top*

Vanilla Nut Caramel
Vanilla caramel and pecans

Rum Nougat
*English walnuts, rum,
raisin, nougat*

Datenut
*Dates, brown sugar
buttercream with English
walnuts and ground
nutmeats on top*

Chelsea
*Chocolate buttercream with
toasted pecans*

Milk Divinity
*Whipped egg whites,
vanilla cream and
English walnuts*

Scotch Kisses
mallow and caramel

Marzipan
Honey almond paste

Café au Lait Truffle
Rich coffee buttercream

Caramel
Caramel with almonds

See's
Famous Old Time
CANDIES

A Sweet Story

See's
Famous Old Time
CANDIES

by Margaret Moos Pick

CHRONICLE BOOKS
SAN FRANCISCO

Library of Congress Cataloging-in-Publication Data:
Pick, Margaret Moos.
    See's famous old time candies : a sweet story / by
Margaret Moos Pick.
       p. cm.
    ISBN: 0-8118-4867-1 (alk. paper)
    1. See's Candies (Firm)—History. 2. Candy indus-
try—United States—Case studies. I. Title.
    HD9330.C654AS446 2005
    338.7'664153'0973—dc22
                                    2004031068

Photo credits: Angela Fafara, Jack Hutcheson,
    and Jon Sandvick
Page 41: Photograph copyright © 2005 by Guittard
    Chocolate Company
Book and cover design by Benjamin Shaykin
Typeset in Monticello CC, Cheltenham BT, Futura BT,
    and Peregroy JF
Manufactured in China

Distributed in Canada by Raincoast Books
9050 Shaughnessy Street
Vancouver, British Columbia V6P 6E5

10 9 8 7 6 5 4 3 2 1

Chronicle Books LLC
85 Second Street
San Francisco, California 94105
www.chroniclebooks.com

See's Candies are available at See's shops in
Arizona, California, Colorado, Hawaii, Idaho,
Illinois, Nevada, New Mexico, Oregon, Utah, and
Washington; as well as Hong Kong and Japan.

See's Candies are also available by phone at
1-800-347-7337, or on the Web at www.sees.com.

Founder Charles A. See (in suit) stands next to his son Laurance, at a gathering of See's employees in Los Angeles, 1941.

This book is dedicated to all of the See's employees—past and present—who have made the world just a little bit sweeter.

Table of Contents

The See's Candies Philosophy

OUR PHILOSOPHY IS QUITE SIMPLE:

Be absolutely persistent in all attitudes regarding quality.

Buy only the best ingredients obtainable.

Offer the most delicious and interesting assortments
of candies possible.

Provide the highest level of customer service in all
aspects of business.

PREFACE

By Warren E. Buffett, Chairman of the Board, See's Candies/Berkshire Hathaway

THE CORPORATE LANDSCAPE OF AMERICA IS LITTERED WITH once-famous brands that have buckled in the heat of a changing world. See's has not only survived, but has prospered for 85 years.

See's is a true wonder. There are very few organizations dealing daily with the public that have maintained their place in the hearts of Americans for as long as See's has. See's Candies' president and CEO, Charles N. (Chuck) Huggins, who has logged over half a century with the company and collected a kit bag full of titles, including maintenance chief and purchasing agent, will tell you that See's is a story of courage, faith, and luck that began in the wilds of Canada when Charles A. See set out to capitalize on his mother's candy recipes. Beyond that, there are two reasons for See's sustained success: people and product. No one has matched our product, and our people are devoted to the proposition that no one will ever match our service, either.

See's is also the story of leadership by Chuck Huggins, an ex–World War II paratrooper and bachelor-of-arts-degree-toting jazz aficionado. Chuck combines the discipline of a fine analytical mind with intuitive marketing savvy and a moral sensibility that is rare in the 21st century. In short, I wish we could clone him.

When Berkshire Hathaway purchased See's Candies in 1972 from the founding family who ran it for 50 years, we were smart enough to ask Chuck to take over the helm. Buying See's was not only a good investment for us, it was a positive learning experience. We discovered that we had purchased a company that held itself to a high standard of business ethics—product quality, service integrity, and the right sort of relationships with employees and suppliers. See's Candies became our model for investment in other quality companies. The long-term results are that Berkshire Hathaway has enjoyed tremendous expansion, and continues to have a special regard for See's Candies, a company that taught us an early and vital lesson about the way to do business.

It has been an enormous pleasure to be associated with this unusual company for all these years. There is so much that is shoddy in the business practices of the world. But not at See's Candies.

By Charles N. Huggins, President and CEO, See's Candies

T HE PAGES OF THIS BOOK BRING FORTH A STORY THAT HAS BEEN told before in many different ways: Immigrant family risks all by leaving their small-town home in order to start a new life in America. My wife Donna encouraged me to authorize this gathering of historic information about the See family's grand adventure in the candy business before it is lost forever.

Though not unusual, See's story is unique in its relationship to the history, growth, and development of western America and California. It is a story of people who came here, saw an opportunity, and took a chance. It is also the story of a man named Charles A. See, a man who believed in himself and had the courage and discipline to make his particular idea become successful.

Charles A. See was also a strong believer in family values. He gained from his mother Mary a sense of honesty, integrity, and the importance of having a reputation for personal trust that carried over into his business dealings. It was these personal attributes that made up Charles's character as he took the risky step of forming See's Candies as a company in 1921. He instilled those same attributes in his family, employees, and business associates throughout the rest of his life, and that is what helped the young company not only survive the great challenges of adversity, but prosper in spite of them.

When Charles passed away in 1949, he left his family the legacy of his character, a new kitchen facility in Los Angeles, and the good luck to be present at the start of a growth cycle in California that was on a par with the Gold Rush 100 years earlier.

Charles's eldest son, Laurance, a Stanford University Class of 1934 graduate, was well prepared to continue to practice the ethics, business principles, and disciplines of his father. He also had, as additional aids to his decision making, the strong business sense and experience of Edward G. Peck, who had been president and general manager of See's operations in northern California since 1936.

I was hired in April 1951 after several interviews with Laurance See and Ed Peck and their wives. My marching orders were simple and straightforward: "Report to Ed Peck at See's San Francisco General Office. You are to learn See's version of how to run a quality candy business." That turned out to be one of the luckiest days of my life.

Ed Peck became my mentor, as it turned out, a man who, while very positive about the ways he expected things to be managed, was willing to turn me loose with a minimum of instruction to see how I might handle problems. And, as time passed, the scope of my responsibilities broadened, along with my knowledge of how See's managed its unique approach to the quality candy business and what it was that caused See's to stand out in comparison to its many competitors.

The certain amount of success I was able to achieve in carrying out my various assignments came to the attention of Laurance See, and I gained his respect. This soon resulted in more important assignments. Between 1954 and 1964 See's was in a hectic growth cycle, opening shops in the many developing shopping malls of that time. In 1957 See's opened a major manufacturing kitchen in South San Francisco.

Twenty years after I joined the company, just after Thanksgiving 1971, I was sitting in my office at our Los Angeles headquarters in deep conversation with three men who were planning to make an offer to the See family to buy the company. They were Warren Buffett, Charlie Munger, and Rick Guerin. Laurance See had died, and the surviving members of the See family had decided to sell all their holdings in the business.

Warren was telling me that if they bought the company, they wanted me to manage See's operations as president and CEO. After negotiations with Laurance's younger brother, Charles B. (Harry), the ownership transfer was completed in January 1972. When I think about lucky days, after more than 30 years of reporting directly to Warren, and secondarily to Charlie, I must rate that event tops. Not only for me, but more importantly for See's as a company and for all our employees. Luck played an important role in the whole transaction.

As the following years have shown, our connection to Berkshire Hathaway, with the incredible business wisdom of Warren and Charlie, has benefited See's as a company and me as its leader in many different ways.

And yet, the main ingredient in the success of the See's organization since 1972 is the dedication and loyalty of its thousands of employees, who have joined us from all walks of life, many serving See's for as long as 25 to 50 years. That alone has made the true difference in See's ability to maintain its enviable position within the confectionery industry.

LEFT: *Assistant General Manager Chuck Huggins reviews shop construction plans in the mid-1950s.*
RIGHT: *Chuck and Donna Huggins, 2004.*

Finally, on a personal note, I have over the years of my long life and many experiences developed a list of outstanding heroes whose courage, character, and intelligence in the conduct of their lives has made a difference to the world and in the conduct of my life. They are: Winston Churchill, Dwight Eisenhower, Harry Truman, Louis Armstrong, and Warren Buffett.

My family has been at the center of my desire to make something of my life. I met my wife Mime while I was attending classes at Kenyon College under the GI Bill in the wake of World War II. Mime and I married in 1947 and headed west in April 1949 in a brand-new Ford V-8 coupe, a wedding gift from her maternal grandmother. Together we shared the great adventure of raising four children: Pete, Anne, Shelley, and Chip, who have given me nine grandchildren. Mime passed away in 1995. In more recent years, the encouragement and support of my wife Donna have made all the difference in the world to me.

And now, as they say, "On with the show." I hope you enjoy this story of the people who created the candy you love.

EVERYONE ASKS US,

"Is Mary See real?"

Absolutely!

PART ONE

Our Founder

Yes, There Is a Real Mary See

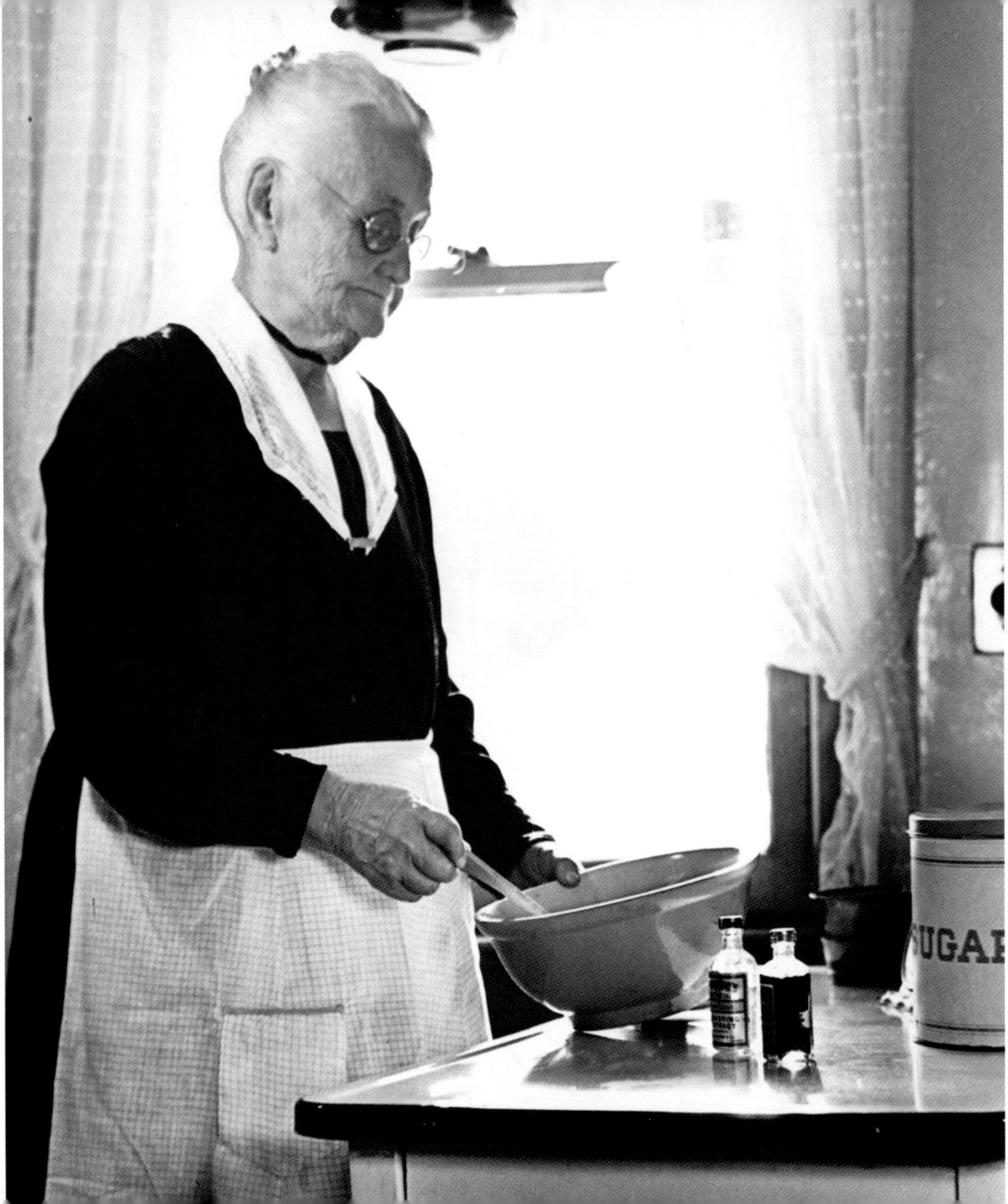

Mary See

WHEN CHARLES A. SEE FOUNDED HIS CANDY COMPANY IN 1921, he didn't need to *invent* a grandmotherly figure to represent See's Candies, as many companies did at the time. (That same year, General Mills came up with the fictional character Betty Crocker as its figurehead.) Charles turned to his mother, Mary See, whose principles inspired his business ethics and whose recipes for candies like Chocolate Walnut Fudge and Victoria Toffee were the cornerstone of his success. He put her picture on every box of chocolates.

Mary See was born Mary Wiseman on September 15, 1854, on Howe Island in an area known as the "1,000 Islands" in the St. Lawrence River in Ontario, Canada. Her father, an immigrant from Ireland, was a farmer. The nearest mainland town was Gananoque, and Mary always thought of "Gan" as her hometown.

She was 20 years old when she married Alexander See, whom she helped run a resort on Tremont Park Island.

Mary had three children. Her son Charles A., the founder of See's Candies, was born in 1882. Her daughter May became a registered nurse, and her daughter Bertha married and lived in Toronto.

Alex See died in 1919, leaving Mary a widow at the age of 64. Though she had never before traveled outside Ontario, she picked up stakes and moved to the Los Angeles area with her son and his family, where they all lived in a pretty post-Victorian bungalow that can still be seen today at 426 South Marengo Street in Pasadena.

We don't know much about Mary See as a person. She didn't leave behind letters or a diary. Like many women of her generation, we can imagine that her life revolved around caring for her family. And, no doubt, making sweets was a pleasant change from the more grueling aspects of housekeeping in the days before labor-saving appliances.

We do know that Mary See took pride in her candy recipes and insisted on only the best ingredients. *Everyone* loved the candies Mary See made in her kitchen. Almost a century after the first See's candy shop opened in 1921, Mary See's recipes are still loved and her picture is still on every box of chocolates.

See family portrait around the turn of the 20th century: Mary See and her husband Alexander (seated center). (L to R): Daughter Bertha, son-in-law Walter Begg, daughter May, and son Charles A. See.

Mary See in her backyard at 426 South Marengo Street, Pasadena.

The See Family in California. (L to R): Mary See, her grandson Laurance, and granddaughter Margaret. Son Charles A. See, founder of See's Candies, holds baby "Harry."

UTH PORCUPINE (Y)

PORCUPINE BURNING JULY 11/11.
COPYRIGHT CANADA
BY H. PETERS. 1911

Charlie & The Chocolate Factory

The Vision of Charles A. See

O UR STORY BEGINS IN THE TOWN OF TIMMINS IN THE SNOWY forests of northern Ontario, where a young man by the name of Charles A. See ran two pharmacies in the Porcupine gold-mining district. His signs proclaiming "Pills and Things" were landmarks in the Canadian wilderness. Charles was fascinated with mining and might have stayed in the frontier forever.

On July 11, 1911, fate intervened. A brutal forest fire swept through the district, burning everything to the ground. Charles waded into nearby Porcupine Lake with his wife to wait out the firestorm. Waves lapped around their necks as the fire raged through town. They were lucky to escape with their lives.

With his pharmacies and home demolished, Charles went looking for work in Toronto. Again, fate intervened. He found a job as the Canadian sales rep for Merckens—one of the oldest chocolate manufacturers in the United States—selling candy-making ingredients in bulk to bakeries, small confectioneries, and to Laura Secord, the popular Canadian candy shops.

Selling chocolate came naturally to Charles. Late in life, he loved to tell the story of how he would work very hard for a couple of days, and then give himself a week off, while he slowly sent the orders he had accumulated in two days of work into headquarters. But Charles soon tired of "the easy life" and began to dream of owning a chain of chocolate shops like the great Canadian chain Laura Secord—but better, and someplace warmer.

Charles turned his attention to the booming economy of Los Angeles in the land of opportunity to the south. He took a chance and traded in the snowdrifts of Canada for the balmy breezes of southern California—2,000 miles away. In the spring of 1920, he left Canada for good with his recently widowed mother, Mary See, his wife Florence, and their two children, Laurance and Margaret.

24

10/11/49

Wafer Cream
100# Conf. AA Sugar
4 gals water
Cook to 236°
add 1 oz Lemon juice
of water. and 20 sheets
Soaked in water.
Cook to 247°

Pour on beater gre[ased]
glycerine. sprinkle
on top of poured [candy]

UNION ⬡ PACIFIC
Road of the Streamliners

Truffle

45# Commander
5# Broc
2½ Gal 36% Cream warm
to body heat.
10# Butter Cream

Melt choc slow
open fire.

10/11/49

WILSHIRE

20# Gran. Sugar
30# Glucose
5 oz. Salt
½ oz. Vanilla
2# Egg Whites
28# Milk Chocolate
1 Bucket Roasted Almonds
4# Butter
Cook 230°

[p]ut mixer and add egg white

[When] beaten & Fluffy, put in kettle
[with] butter that has been mixed with
[choc]olate (milk). Then add Almonds
[Leave] in kettle over night and dip in
milk chocolate.

See's
Famous Home Made
CANDIES

NET WEIGHT THREE POUNDS   COPYRIGHTED 1922

IT WAS A TIME WHEN MOVIES WERE SILENT, WHISKEY WAS OUTLAWED, & CHOCOLATES COST ABOUT 50 CENTS A POUND . . .

People had plenty to celebrate in 1921. The Great War had ended in victory a few years earlier, and the economy was on a roll. You could buy a Model T Ford for $300, and suddenly everybody had to have one.

Hemlines jumped from ankle length to above the knee. Flappers kicked up their heels to hot jazz tunes like "Wang, Wang Blues." There was this new thing called radio, and Rudolph Valentino was vamping it up as *The Sheik* on the silver screen.

Though business was booming in L.A., Charles See faced stiff competition from the hundreds of confectioners already in business when he arrived with his dream of building a chain of sweet shops.

Clearly, he needed something special to distinguish his product from the rest. So Charles founded See's Candies on two principles that would never be compromised—his mother's recipes and the finest butter, cream, chocolate, fruits, and nuts that money could buy. He was so devoted to quality that his suppliers added a new phrase to their sales jargon: "See's Quality," which was above "Top Quality."

It was a time in America when people tried a little harder to do their best. Charles transformed his mother's pioneer spirit, her recipes, and her desire for quality into a way of doing business that was "just a little bit better" than the competition. With his mother as the symbol on every box of chocolates, he knew what he had to live up to.

In 1921, Charles See found a financial backer and opened up the first See's candy shop at 135 Western Avenue North in Los Angeles. In the back of the shop, there was a candy kitchen where the recipes that he had enjoyed as a child were made with the same care as in his mother's kitchen. The original recipes that Mary See created are still available today—Chocolate Walnut Fudge, Victoria Toffee, Hand-Dipped Bon Bons, and Maple Walnut Creams.

It wasn't long before customers began to notice that See's Candies tasted as good as homemade sweets—and that the price was affordable. Sales began to take off.

Shops opened in the Grauman's Chinese Theatre building and in Pasadena on Colorado Boulevard. By 1925, there were a dozen See's candy shops across Los Angeles.

Yet for every success that Charles See enjoyed, he faced an equal number of challenges. In 1929, the stock-market crash closed banks and wiped out thousands of family businesses. By 1932, 13 million people—25 percent of the workforce—were unemployed in the United States. See's Candies might now be only a footnote to history if it weren't for Charles's foresight—and his good luck.

In 1931, luck walked in the door in the form of a tall, lanky Canadian by the name of Edward G. Peck, who was looking for work.

Charles See had the intelligence and work ethic to make the most of his good fortune. In a letter written in 1976, Ed Peck described the strategy Charles developed to survive the decade-long Depression: "In 1929 everyone in L.A. sold candies at 80 cents a pound, but when the big Depression hit us, Mr. See reduced his price to 60 cents a pound. Then 50 cents a pound. Nobody else cut prices like that.

In the mid-1920s, See's experimented with selling ice cream.

Ed Peck worked for See's competitor, Mary Fraser Candies, a block away from See's first shop. When the Depression hit, Mary Fraser folded, and Peck moved down the street, where he began his 41-year career at See's.

26

"We had to reduce wages to rock bottom. And Mr. See visited all his landlords and told them, 'Lower rent is better than no rent. Reduce the rent to See's and we'll survive together.' They cooperated in a savings of over $10,000 a year to See's."

Charles See traveled the country, intently observing the competition and looking for ways to make See's Candies better. In April 1932, during the worst of the Depression, Charles wrote a letter to Sales Manager Ed Peck from the Hotel Stevens in Chicago, telling him how their two biggest competitors there were handling the rocky economy. Fanny May had slashed prices below cost, and Martha Washington had closed a dozen stores.

Gala opening of See's "Sunlit Candy Studio" in Los Angeles, 1931.

In these hard times, Charles See made three bold moves.

While the competition was letting the quality of their candy slide, Charles took a different approach. He created new sources of revenue and developed unusual marketing tools. In November 1932, he decided to sell his candy at a bulk-rate price of 42.5 cents a pound in quantities over 50 pounds, prepaid, offering a discount on quantity sales. It was a radical idea. No one else in the industry was doing anything like it, and it became the prototype for See's present-day Quantity Discount Program.

In spite of the tough economy in Los Angeles, Charles forged ahead with plans to debut See's "Sunlit Candy Studio," a new concept in the making and marketing of candy. This innovative shop and kitchen with the latest equipment made it possible for See's confections to be created in full view of the public through huge plate-glass windows, assuring customers of the candy's purity. To maximize publicity, Charles tied the gala opening to the company's support of the 1932 Olympic Games about to take place in the city. On November 24, 1931, Hollywood celebrities and eager crowds converged on the studio for an open house. Searchlights lit up the sky and music filled the air.

Everywhere else the competition was closing stores, but in 1936 Charles See sent Ed Peck to San Francisco to open new shops, expanding See's operations outside the Los Angeles area for the first time. Charles thought of Ed as a member of the family, and sent him off to handle the expansion in the City by the Bay on his own, with a pat on the back and the advice to "be successful."

Four years later, Ed Peck had 18 "Mary See's Dainty White Shops" going strong all over the Bay Area, and as far away as San Jose to the south and Sacramento to the north. And in December 1940, at a cost of $100,000, See's Candies opened a new 15,000-square-foot facility at the corner of Market and Valencia streets in San Francisco.

General Manager Ed Peck launched a flashy promotion to showcase the opening. Radio spots and newspaper ads invited the public to tour the building to see its state-of-the-art equipment, taste the candy, and enjoy up-to-the-minute amenities like air conditioning!

On opening night, lights lit up the façade of the building and beamed out into the foggy night. Eight thousand people enjoyed the See family's hospitality. While

VIPs attended a private reception, the general public swarmed through the candy kitchen as a full staff of white-uniformed candy workers were kept busy making and serving candy to the guests.

LEFT: *Thousands tour See's San Francisco candy kitchen on opening night in 1940.*
RIGHT: *In this family snapshot, used in See's advertisements, Mary See's grandson "Harry" enjoys the chocolates.*

A FAMILY STORY

Charles See led his company through economic disaster and the upheaval of World War II to accomplish substantial growth. He grew the business from one store in Los Angeles to 78 shops throughout California, with 2,000 employees.

By the end of the 1930s, the younger generation of the See family began to make its mark in the company. Laurance See was only 9 years old when the first See's candy shop opened in 1921. By the mid-'30s, he had graduated from Stanford University and become General Manager of See's Los Angeles operation.

Mary See, who had inspired her son to create a successful business based on her candy recipes, passed away in 1939 at the age of 85. Charles See lived for a decade after his mother's death.

From Easy Rider to the Internet

Who Was That Man on the Motorcycle?

Pining for chocolate?

How would you like to pick up the phone and have your order hand-delivered? Well, you can. See's has offered mail-order delivery around the world since the 1920s, now delivering 1,400,926 pounds of candy each year by mail. You can even satisfy your hunger for chocolate with a click of the mouse by ordering on the Web. But in 1928, a messenger in a snappy uniform would ring your doorbell with your candies in hand.

In the Roaring Twenties, Los Angeles was a boomtown, mining the newly minted gold of the bustling film industry in the Hollywood Hills.

Hugh Fry rode through the ranks to become part of See's top management team.

If a dashing film star or cigar-chomping mogul wanted to bestow an extra-fancy heart-shaped box of the best chocolates in town on his favorite starlet, he'd ring up his local See's Candies shop. At company headquarters, they'd pick up the call and Hugh Fry would slip out of his persona as shipping clerk, don his chauffeur's outfit, jump on See's customized Harley Davidson motorcycle, and buzz across town to deliver the goods.

The cute little cottage with lace curtains built over the Harley's sidecar would turn heads as Hugh cruised down Pico or Santa Monica Boulevard. And it looked impressive parked at the curb as Hugh strode to the door of the lucky starlet's bungalow—carrying a red velvet, heart-shaped box of See's homemade chocolates.

The idea of motorcycle deliveries originated when founder Charles See took an equipment-buying trip to Europe, where he saw deliveries being made by motorcycles with sidecars. Charles thought the idea would work well in L.A.—with the added bonus of being a mobile billboard.

(Note to motorcycle aficionados—the very first motorbikes See's used for deliveries were Indians, not Harleys.)

3. MUST CHECK YES ☐ NO ☐ FOR CARD ENCLOSED.
4. INSERT CARD COMPLETELY IN BOX
5. DATE AND INITIAL
6. SLIDE BOX ON BELT - DO NOT LIFT.

6. SLIDE BOX ON BELT - DO NOT LIFT.

2 lb
Milk

3 lb
Milk

5 lb
Milk

Mail-order procedures at See's Candies have evolved over the years through a methodical process of research and development, keeping up with innovations in technology—and sometimes old-fashioned, seat-of-the-pants trial and error.

Vice President of Marketing Dick Van Doren, a 45-year veteran of the company, tells this story:

"In my opinion, we now have a first-rate operation. We are constantly testing new packaging techniques—which reminds me of an interesting testing procedure that we had in the early days of our mail-order department. I call it the 'Mary Lund procedure.'

"Mary Lund was the foreperson in charge of our mail-order department, and she ran a very tight ship. Her husband Carl was our shipping manager, and they were both very dedicated employees. One day in October 1971, I visited the mail-order department to see if everything was ready for the holiday season. From a distance, I could see Mary winding up like a baseball pitcher and throwing a box of candy in a mailing carton at someone or something!

"By the time I entered the department, she had thrown three more boxes at a blank wall a good 15 feet away. I said, 'Mary, what in the heck are you doing?' She replied, 'Oh, this is our testing procedure to see if we have enough protective wadding in each box, because this is the way the post office handles our product.'

"You can imagine that I got a big chuckle over this, and told Mary that we should find a better way of testing. As she prepared for another throw, she replied, 'When you come up with a better test, let me know.'

"We did come up with a better testing method. But not until after Mary retired!"

The San Francisco mail-order processing room in the 1960s.

33

PART TWO

The Candy

Quality Without Compromise
Since 1921

See's All-Star Hit Parade

POUND BY POUND, THESE CONFECTIONS WEIGH IN AS SEE'S top hits. If you can't find your favorite on the list, it's no wonder, with 150 varieties to choose from!

✳ Almond Clusters ✳
Roasted almonds enrobed in See's milk or dark chocolate

✳ Butterscotch Lollypops ✳
Rich butterscotch hard candy on a stick

✳ Butterscotch Square ✳
Soft center of brown sugar buttercream and vanilla

✳ Café au Lait Truffle ✳
Rich buttercream with blended coffee and cream

✳ Chelsea ✳
Soft center with chocolate buttercream and pecans

✳ Chocolate Lollypops ✳
Gourmet chocolate hard candy on a stick

Chelsea

Dark Butterchew

❋ Dark Butterchew ❋
See's trademark vanilla, brown sugar caramel with dark European-style
chocolate coating

❋ Dark Chocolate Chip Truffle ❋
Rich buttercream flavored with semi-sweet chocolate with chocolate chips inside

❋ Dark Chocolate Truffle ❋
Rich buttercream with semi-sweet chocolate and chopped nuts
and milk chocolate on top

❋ Dark Nougat ❋
Chewy nougat with honey, roasted almonds, and coconut

❋ Key Lime Truffle ❋
Rich buttercream with key lime purée and white chocolate

❋ King Caramel ❋
Chewy caramel, crunchy almonds, and milk chocolate

❋ Marzipan ❋
Almond paste blended with honey

❋ Milk Bordeaux ❋
See's traditional confection with brown sugar and buttercream inside,
milk chocolate outside, and chocolate "sprinkles" on top

Dark Nougat

King Caramel

Milk Bordeaux

✻ Milk/Dark Chocolate Butter Cream ✻
Soft center flavored with chocolate buttercream, butter, and vanilla

✻ Milk Patties ✻
Chewy vanilla caramel

✻ Molasses Chips ✻
Crispy molasses honeycomb and chocolate

✻ Peanut Brittle ✻
Crunchy and buttery, with whole peanuts plus a few secret ingredients

✻ Raspberry Truffle ✻
Rich buttercream, flavored with raspberries and dark chocolate

✻ Scotchmallow ✻
Layers of honey marshmallow and rich caramel covered in dark chocolate

✻ Toffee-ettes ✻
Bite-size butter brickle pieces drenched in milk chocolate
and studded with toasted almond bits

✻ Walnut Square ✻
English walnuts with a chewy vanilla caramel

There are so many candies to choose from, for the sweetest dreams, you could start counting See's Candies instead of sheep. *Raspberry Creams . . . Cashew Brittle . . . Apricot Delight . . . Almond Royal . . . Vanilla Nut Fudge . . . Molasses Chips . . . Polar Bear Paws . . .* You get the idea. Then again, you might forget about sleep.

Scotchmallow

Raspberry Truffle

Marshmints

Marshmints sound like they might be flora or fauna straight out of the Okefenokee Swamp—Georgia's natural wetland habitat.

But Marshmints are actually See's candy pieces. Bright green mint jelly, honey marshmallow, and dark chocolate make it nectar of the gods to its fans.

There is more to the Marshmints story than meets the taste buds. See's Candies produced the first Marshmints in the 1940s, and all was well for 40 years. Then in the 1980s, managers in See's shops began to run out of space in their display cases for all the new candies that had come along.

Chuck Huggins, who took over as president in 1972, was informed of the situation. He asked the managers to provide him with a list of the least popular pieces in their shops. Responses varied, but there was a general consensus that the world could survive without Marshmints.

Marshmints were discontinued—until Chuck Huggins received this letter.

Dear Sirs:

It seems so bleak since they left, so empty. I walk listlessly through my days wondering if I will ever see their bright green eyes again . . . I am heartbroken, deprived of my only true love . . . MARSHMINTS! I hereby submit my plea for Marshmints to return forever!

Sincerely,
Mousie Zavala
Martinez, California

Some CEOs might have read the letter, chuckled, and tossed it out—but not Chuck Huggins. He couldn't resist engineering a happy ending.

Marshmints made a comeback, and the Marshmint Club was founded. Everyone who buys the candy is now automatically enrolled and receives a bright green membership card, the club newsletter, and a handsome gold and green pin. (Not available in stores, Marshmints can be special-ordered by mail, or on the Web.)

Dear Marshmint Club Member:

Attached you will find your one-of-a-kind Marshmint Club pin. Please accept this as a token of our appreciation for your enthusiasm and support of our Marshmint Club.

Sincerely,
See's CANDIES

A Chocolate Lover's Fantasy

IMAGINE A SPARKLING STAINLESS-STEEL TANKER TRUCKLOAD OF chocolate making a routine stop at your door. It's all in a day's business for See's Candies. A tour of the candy kitchens in both South San Francisco and Los Angeles begins in the parking lot, where even the pavement is swept as clean as Mary See's front porch.

What immediately catches the eye is the 50-foot-long tanker truck with a payload of Guittard Milk Chocolate—that's 52,000 pounds of chocolate!

The Guittard tanker is met in the parking lot by See's Quality Assurance team, decked out in white lab coats and hairnets. The QA team runs an extensive range of lab tests, checking for food safety and doing sensory analysis before the chocolate is accepted for use at See's kitchens. Samples of chocolate are drawn from the top *and* bottom of the tanker. Like a connoisseur of fine wine, the lab technician first sniffs the samples to make sure they have the proper "notes" of chocolate. If not, they are turned away.

Then the QA team does a thorough check of temperature and viscosity. The last thing you want is 52,000 pounds of cooling chocolate to firm up and clog the system. And if the liquid chocolate is too thin, it will not coat the candy well.

A giant hose is attached to a pumping station built into See's candy kitchen, and the rich scent of warm milk chocolate fills the air. For two-and-a-half hours, the tanker truck pumps its treasure trove of chocolate into See's massive holding tanks. Good to the last drop and expensive to boot, the final hundred pounds of liquid chocolate are squeegeed through the discharge port.

See's El Camino Real and La Cienega Boulevard candy kitchens each hold 200,000 pounds of melted chocolate. In the Christmas season, when the place is hopping, there may be two tanker trucks pumping chocolate into the building at the same time—while a third truck waits across the street to pull in.

A TASTE OF CHOCOLATE

Imagine tasting chocolate for a living! It's all part of the job for the Quality Assurance team at See's Candies. Just as the quality of fine wine begins in the vineyard, the quality of fine chocolate begins with the cacao pods, which contain the cocoa beans. The cocoa Guittard uses to make the chocolate it provides to See's is a custom blend created from cocoa beans gathered from top growing areas around the world. Guittard takes the extra step of aging its dark and milk chocolate for months prior to use. This adds yet another dimension of flavor, making See's chocolates taste "smoother" and "rounder" than others.

When sampling, See's chocolate tasters talk in terms of "flavor notes": They taste *and* smell for balanced notes of caramel, malt, dairy, chocolate, and cocoa in samples taken from the 52,000-pound batches of chocolate See's purchases from the Guittard Chocolate Company. Tasters also watch out for "off notes"—smoky, "hammy," minty, or even rubbery flavors. Chocolate, like fine wine, is highly absorbent. Stored next to goods with a strong aroma, it may pick up the taste.

See's dark chocolate has a rich deep brown—almost black—color with a high-gloss shine. Light reflects off the chocolate much as it would off a mirror. The aroma of See's dark chocolate is pungent, with notes of chocolate fudge and vanilla in the bouquet. And there is a distinctive "snap" felt when biting into it.

See's milk chocolate has a rich red-brown color and the same high-gloss shine. Its flavor profile is complex, with layers of chocolate, malt, and caramel, and a finish of cream and cocoa. It, too, "snaps" when you bite into it.

See's white chocolate has a pure ivory color plus the characteristic high-gloss shine of all See's chocolates. The shine is an indicator that See's uses cocoa butter in its white chocolate. Another indicator is the distinctive "chocolate" flavor note that is lacking in most other white chocolates. Lesser white chocolates substitute inexpensive fat sources for cocoa butter.

The Guittard Chocolate Company has a relationship with See's that goes back more than half a century. The company was founded in San Francisco by a young Frenchman and chocolate artisan, Etienne Guittard, more than 130 years ago. Etienne's grandson, Horace A. Guittard, graduated from Stanford University in the class of 1934, the same class as Laurance See, the son of See's founder Charles See. By the early 1950s, both Laurance and Horace found themselves running their family business, and decided it would be natural to do business together.

Today, the Guittard Chocolate Company provides the vital function of delivering high-quality finished chocolate to See's ready for use as "chocolate coating" and flavoring.

In 1959, See's made history in the confectionery business as the first company to come up with the idea of delivering melted chocolate via tanker truck, ready to use. Now, both milk and dark chocolate are delivered to See's candy kitchens in liquid form.

"Our relationship of more than 50 years with See's has made us a better company. They ask us to do things that no other customer asks us—like requiring a lot more tasting and aging of the chocolate—and we are happy to do it. See's keeps us on our toes." —Gary Guittard, president of Guittard Chocolate

43

Candy Making Now & Then

MADE TODAY THE OLD-FASHIONED WAY & THE MOST MODERN WAY

HOW DO YOU MAKE 800 MILLION PIECES OF CANDY EACH YEAR taste like they just came out of Mary See's kitchen?

1. Take 1,400,000 pounds of Challenge Grade AA creamery butter. (Accept no substitutes. No margarine allowed!)

2. Combine with 4,000,000 pounds of fresh heavy cream

3. Add 7,500,000 pounds of C & H Pure Cane Sugar from Hawaii. (No cane juice need apply.)

4. Caramelize slowly in copper kettles at 248°F on an open fire or in precision, high-tech computerized continuous cookers

5. Cover with more than 10,000,000 pounds of Guittard chocolate—your choice of milk, dark, semi-sweet, or white chocolate

6. Add 4,000,000 pounds of top-quality California-grown almonds and English walnuts, and peanuts, cashews, and pecans

7. Mix in, as needed, 400,000 pounds of fresh freeze-dried blueberries, strawberries, raspberries, oranges, key lime, Granny Smith apples, and Hawaiian pineapple prepared by Oregon Freeze Dry

8. Add chopped apricots, Khadrawy dates, and whole cherries as required

9. Feed in honey marshmallow and peanut butter

10. Flavor with vanilla from Madagascar, peppermint, top-grade Canadian maple sugar, honey, zesty lemon, and rich coffee

11. Garnish with toasted Angel Flake coconut and Ruby Red raisins

12. Apply old-world craftsmanship by experienced candy makers

13. Combine with the best modern technology

14. Test constantly for taste, quality, and safety

15. Pack each piece individually by hand

OPPOSITE: *Candy makers add whole cherries to a batch of Mayfair cream in a cream beater, a piece of equipment that is much the same today as it was in the 1930s.*

The Nut Room

The rich aroma of gently toasting almonds greets visitors as they climb the stairs to the nut-roasting room, where Gregorio Vallejo hefts a 50-pound carton of shelled almonds onto his shoulder and feeds the raw nuts into a hopper that funnels them into a nut roaster. Below, workers double-check and sort the various nuts used in See's products. Checking *and double-checking* all the ingredients that come into the candy kitchens is one of the things that the people at See's are a little "nutty" about, and they don't quite trust anyone else to take the same care they do.

It works like this:

* First, See's selects the best and most trusted suppliers.
* Then, See's Purchasing and Quality Assurance teams make regular inspection visits to the processing and manufacturing facilities of each supplier.
* Ingredients from the suppliers are checked again when they are delivered.
* Before use in See's candy kitchens, QA lab technicians carefully examine every delivery for microbiologic compliance and purity, and to make sure the delivery meets See's specifications in terms of size and quality.

When it comes to product quality at See's, nothing is left to chance!

Haig Berberian personifies the integrity and relentless eye for quality of the suppliers that See's has been blessed to work with through the years. Haig and his brother Jimmy escaped from war-torn Armenia as teenagers in the early part of the 20th century and immigrated to the United States, where they built a small empire in Modesto, California, buying and shelling quality walnuts.

Recalling his meeting Haig for the first time, Chuck Huggins says: "I had recently become the purchasing manager for See's, and Ed Peck asked me to get to know our suppliers out in the field. It was a blazing hot afternoon in the Central Valley in 1954 when I pulled up next to an enormous tin building. As I got out of my car, I saw a man in a suit and tie with a stylish fedora on his head standing on the loading dock going through sacks of walnuts in the shell. It was Haig, checking the quality of the walnuts he was about to buy. I would soon find out that Haig did all of his business on a handshake, that he knew everything there was to know

ABOVE: *"Walnut King"*
Haig Berberian and
Chuck Huggins at
the 1977 opening of a
See's store in Modesto,
California.
RIGHT: *See's Candies*
Quality Assurance lab
is an industry leader in
food safety.

about walnuts, and that I could trust him 100 percent to deliver the best-tasting and best-looking nuts to See's—at the best price."

The success of See's Candies has always been tied to its historic relationships with suppliers who, like Haig Berberian, share See's belief in quality ingredients. From the 1930s on, the Slate family has supplied See's with almonds from their family operation near Paso Robles, California. Both Lew Slate and Haig Berberian, the "Walnut King," were known for their honesty, their knowledge of their product, and their market savvy. These two like-minded, legendary figures, revered for the way they conducted their business, joined forces in the almond-shelling business in the northern San Joaquin Valley, supplying See's Candies with quality nuts and advising the company on market trends.

Copper Kettles

See's trademark buttercream tastes great for a very good reason. Sugar, cream, and other ingredients are caramelized at 248°F in Paul Bunyan–size copper kettles over a gas flame. At the magic moment when each batch is ready, two candy makers transport the kettle on a special dolly to a machine known as a "cream beater." There, as the mixture cools, bricks of top-grade Challenge butter are broken into chunks by hand and dropped into the rich, warm caramel to melt.

Depending on what type of candy is being made, walnuts, almonds, or pecans, cherries or berries, or flavorings of vanilla, orange, or maple are added next. The cream beaters fold these ingredients into the candy mixture until it forms a gorgeous mass of buttercream—ready to be shaped into candy pieces and enrobed with dark, semi-sweet, white, or milk chocolate. Each candy maker takes pride in his work and can tell by smell or sight when the mixture is ready for each step.

Many of See's candies are still made in small "hand batches" using the same recipes and, in many cases, methods that have been used for decades. But since the 1970s, See's has been a technology leader in the confectionery industry, utilizing improvements in candy-making equipment by European manufacturers that make it possible for the company to provide its customers with an even better, more consistent product, place a greater emphasis on food safety, and create better working conditions for See's candy makers.

The Porcupine & Tweety Bird

In another room, a giant computerized continuous cooker makes precision batches of peanut brittle, saving back-breaking labor on the part of the candy makers.

Affectionately known as "Mr. Peanut Brittle," Pedro Ramos has been at the See's Los Angeles candy kitchen for 45 years. His job used to involve intense manual labor. Now, that part of his work can be accomplished with new, custom-designed equipment, which he has been trained to operate. But nothing can replace Mr. Peanut Brittle's experience and skill. Regarding the improvements in candy-making equipment, Chuck Huggins says, "We modernize the processes, but we never change the recipes, or the ingredients!"

"The Porcupine" and "Tweety Bird" have revolutionized the making of Peanut Brittle, Victoria Toffee, and all the other "brittles" at See's. Two See's Research

48

OPPOSITE:
Photographer Jon Sandvick developed a new look for See's in the 1970s with production shots like this one; and also giant blow-ups of candy pieces used on shop window display cards.

OPPOSITE: *In the 1930s, food safety apparel like hairnets and gloves were unheard of. And women with machetes did the work that would later be performed by Tweety Bird.*
BELOW LEFT: *Tweety Bird is the first robot in See's candy kitchens.*
BELOW RIGHT: *The equipment that produces See's new Awesome Peanut Brittle Bar is as amazing as the bar itself—it can make over 1,000 pounds of candy an hour.*

and Development managers, Les Curtin and Greg Ward, created the equipment designs after extensive research in Italy, Germany, and the United States.

The Porcupine simultaneously cooks and stirs the brittle mixture with enormous hollow prongs filled with steam heat, which are attached to a rotating drum. As the hot, buttery brittle comes out of the Porcupine, it is laid down on a chilled stainless-steel belt, and cools quickly.

The brittle next comes under the command of Tweety Bird, a bright yellow robotic arm holding a large stainless-steel paddle. Capable of sensing the appropriate length of each piece, Tweety Bird slices and then flips the slabs of brittle, allowing them to cool on both sides. In a final maneuver, Tweety Bird cleverly cleans the stainless-steel paddle with one swipe.

Next, the brittle passes into a long cooling tunnel. It emerges ready to be enrobed in chocolate, except for Peanut Brittle, which goes straight to the packing room.

51

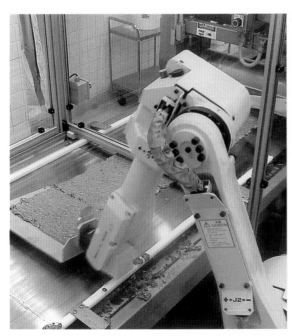

The Enrobing Room

Each year, See's "enrobes" 23 million pounds of candy in chocolate. Buttercreams, nuts, chews, and other candies enter the enrobing room to receive their coat of chocolate via enclosed conveyor belts. Workers guide the candy pieces as they come down onto the enrobing belts, sorting out any that are even slightly misshapen.

The perfectly shaped candies march in lines of 20 down the enrobing belt. Sollich, the largest manufacturer of chocolate coating systems in the world, supplies See's with this key piece of equipment. The "enrober" generously paints the bottoms of the candy pieces with chocolate, and then smothers the tops and sides with more melted chocolate. It does this maneuver again and again, until a layer of chocolate coats every millimeter of the candy pieces. Whether milk, dark, semi-sweet, or white, the melted chocolate must be kept at just the right temperature and thickness or it will not firm up properly to create a smooth, glossy coat. Finally, the candy pieces with their chocolate "robes" pass through long, covered cooling tunnels.

At the end of the line, workers carefully sort the individual pieces again, setting aside any that are imperfect. The majority of the candies are then mechanically assembled onto layer cards and placed into stock boxes. Later, shrink-wrapped

Seventy-six percent of all the candy See's makes today is chocolate-coated.

1950s

2005

pallets of stock boxes will be delivered to See's packing departments and distribution warehouses. In the packing departments, each piece of candy is packed by hand in a brown parchment "crinkle cup," boxed by assortment, wrapped, and sent off to meet the world.

THE BON BON DEPARTMENT

There is happy chatter as the ladies in the Bon Bon Department go about their business, hand-rolling and hand-dipping a mind-boggling 180,000 pounds of Bon Bons every year.

WHAT EXACTLY IS A BONBON?

It's an old-fashioned candy—one of the first recipes that Mary See introduced in her son's candy shops. The center of each bonbon is filled with a rich buttercream, studded with apricots, black walnuts, coconut, maple sugar, fresh oranges, caramel, or English walnuts. First, the filling for each candy is rolled by hand into a round or football-like shape. Then each candy is dipped in a rich fondant cream using a custom tool that looks a little like a crochet hook. Some are topped off with pecans.

Hand-rolling and hand-dipping bonbons is an art form that has been preserved at See's Candies for 80 years or more, passed down from generation to generation among the women who work in the Bon Bon Department. The pastel-pink, yellow, orange,

53

and maple-sugar-beige Bon Bons all have a distinctive swirl on top that can only be achieved by a practiced hand.

Bon Bons are so cute they look like they might kick up their heels and dance on the top of a prettily decorated table—maybe the Bon Bon Can-Can!

ABOVE: *See's Bon Bons are crafted as carefully today as they were in the 1930s.*

The Lollypop Guild

You don't have to take a trip to the land of Oz to meet our "Lollypop Guild." You can find them at work at See's Rollins Road Lollypop Factory in Burlingame, California.

Sovann Sok shepherds a butterscotch lollypop batch down the line. Butter and cream give See's Lollypops and Little Pops their smooth, rich texture.

You're first. Dive in.

Quality Uncompromised

"USE IT UP, WEAR IT OUT, MAKE DO, OR DO WITHOUT" WAS A way of life for Americans in the '40s. Everything changed the day Japan attacked the U.S. Pacific Fleet at Pearl Harbor on December 7, 1941. The United States went on total war footing. Men of all ages enlisted in military service. Americans were issued ration cards for basic necessities of life like gasoline, butter, sugar, meat, coffee, shoes, and tires. Blackouts were a daily routine for people living near the coast.

Many of See's employees went off to war, including Laurance and Harry See. With so many workers in the military, it was a challenge for the company to keep production and operations running smoothly. An even greater challenge was how to keep making quality candies when butter and sugar and cream were rationed and in extremely short supply.

There were heated discussions within the company as to how See's could stay in business without changing the ingredients in its recipes or reducing the quantity of rationed goods like butter, cream, and sugar that were used in the recipes. It was a time of hard decisions.

Ed Peck was horrified at the thought of tampering with the ingredients and running the risk of reducing the quality of See's Candies. In a letter he wrote in 1942, Peck argues that it would be better to completely discontinue making Victoria Toffee and California Brittle rather than to reduce the amount of butter used in each batch and destroy the flavor. Butter was in such short supply that the ration he received for the whole week would have normally been used in one day of prewar operation.

In the end, Ed Peck came up with a clever idea, and See's management decided to take a chance on his radical plan. Instead of compromising the quality of the candy, See's rationed the candy allotted to the shops. Using the best ingredients, they made less candy. Each shop received a quota to sell, and when they ran out of candy after a few hours, they closed the shops. In an era of Spam and oleomargarine, when there were so few "quality" foodstuffs available, people were willing to wait in long lines to buy See's Candies because the company chose to live up to its motto: *Quality Without Compromise.*

The See family bet the future of the company on a gamble that customers would value their choice of quality over quantity when they decided not to change Mary See's recipes and elected to maintain the high quality of their confections. People were so delighted to be able to purchase candies made with real butter and chocolate that they didn't object when the shops ran out of goods and closed early. In keeping with the times, the company urged customers to "be conservative in their See's candy purchases and buy more War Bonds."

Postwar Expansion & Construction

C ALIFORNIA WAS BOOMING IN THE POSTWAR ECONOMY OF THE 1950s. Mom, Dad, the kids, and the dog jumped in the Chevy and headed west, leaving behind the cornfields of Iowa and Minnesota in search of sunshine and a "ranch home" in the California suburban dream.

See's Candies expanded with the times. After Laurance See became president of the company when his father passed away in 1949, he fulfilled his father's vision of building new, modern candy-making facilities in both Los Angeles and San Francisco. Laurance had a reputation as a modest and patient man who listened carefully and made the right decisions to grow the company.

By the mid-'50s, construction was underway on a new candy-making facility for northern California. Today, the See's facility at 210 El Camino Real in South San Francisco houses the corporate offices of the company and a candy kitchen that produces 16 million pounds of confections a year.

BELOW, LEFT: *Laurance See at the La Cienega construction site in Los Angeles in the 1940s.*
BELOW, RIGHT: *In 1949, when See's candy-making facility in Los Angeles was new, it was surrounded by beet fields, not freeways like today.*

"And While You're at It, Come Up with a Name!"

CHARLES SEE STARTED HIS COMPANY WITH HIS MOTHER'S recipes for Chocolate Walnut Fudge, Peanut Brittle, Victoria Toffee, and Maple Walnut Creams. But as time went on, he came up with his own candy creations, too.

New ideas for candy pieces have always come from the people who work at See's. Drenched in the rich aromas of melted chocolate and butterscotch that waft through the building, and surrounded by all that sweet cream, honey, and nuts, they're naturally inspired to dream up something new—and delicious.

Ed Peck, who was general manager of See's San Francisco operation from the mid-'30s through the '60s, was no exception. Among the candies he helped develop were Almond Royals and the "Beverly" filling used in Bon Bons and Easter Eggs.

An outgoing man, Peck loved to travel around town and drop in on other people in the candy business. There were at least a dozen confectioners operating in the Bay Area at the time, and each had only a few stores. Blum's was popular in San Francisco. Wilson's Confectioners, run by a fellow nicknamed "Sticky Wilson," touted itself as "a candy with a college education." Both had stores close to See's shops.

See's president, Chuck Huggins, recalls Ed Peck's stories about how he kept tabs on the competition in the early days:

"Ed Peck scouted all the local confectioners. He was a great talker, and as he chatted with the managers, he'd investigate what kind of candy everyone was making—what was popular, and what was not. He'd take the managers and their wives out to dinner at the finest restaurants. All the while, Peck would be sitting there scribbling away with a notebook on his knee as everyone else was eating and drinking. Pretty soon, he'd be hiring candy makers away from the competition. Then he'd go to New York and do the same thing there, and then on to Chicago.

"He'd come back here and call Milt Rigby, then our head candy

OPPOSITE: *See's employee Christmas party, San Francisco, 1943. General Manager Ed Peck (left) sits on the floor next to his son, Laurance (Larry) Peck.*
RIGHT: *Almond Royals.*

maker. 'Hey, Milt, go down and cook up a batch of this and see if we've got it right. And while you're at it, think up a name for it.'"

See's latest offering, the Awesome Peanut Brittle Bar, was recently developed by a couple of candy makers in the Los Angeles candy kitchen. For years, they had been making up a small batch of milk-chocolate-covered peanut brittle right before the weekend to share with their fellow employees. It soon became an underground hit with See's employees, and the new product was brought to the attention of Chuck Huggins. When he was presented with a sample to taste, the word "Awesome!" was scrawled on the side of the cardboard box it came in. One bite was all it took. It was thumbs up on the new candy bar, which would be dubbed the "Awesome Bar."

Chuck Huggins has helped develop several new candies for See's, including one popular piece composed of chocolate buttercream studded with toasted pecans and covered with milk chocolate. The light chocolate frappé flavor with its hint of toasted pecans is reminiscent to Chuck of "a special Christmas cake." Candy makers carefully adjusted the cream's flavors, and the piece was in development at See's for months. As fate would have it, when the team finally decided the candy was ready for production, Huggins and his wife, Mime, were on vacation in London. The last item on the agenda was a name. One afternoon, after a trip to the Mechanics Museum, Huggins was standing in a red phone box in Chelsea, brainstorming with the team back in California. While they talked, his gaze fell on the bustling streets full of fashionable shoppers and he said, "Why not call it Chelsea?"

ABOVE: *Awesome Peanut Brittle Bar.*
LEFT: *Chelsea.*
OPPOSITE: *1930s-era cream beater.*

The Story of Truffles

The phone rang one morning in 1977 in Chuck Huggins's Los Angeles office. The voice on the other end of the line was forceful and obviously intelligent. "I am fascinated by See's Candies. I want to have a chat with you because I think I can help you. At one time, I was deeply involved in developing the process of 'quick freezing' baked goods that made a name for Sara Lee. When can we meet?" It was Charlie Lubin, retired CEO of Sara Lee Bakeries, a division of Consolidated Foods.

Bemused by the call, Huggins agreed to meet him the following week. The outcome of their four-hour conversation was Lubin's recommendation that See's hire a Dutch engineer by the name of Hans Van Eikeren to help the company develop new technologies to better

Truffles
for that special occasion

compete in the confectionery business.

Huggins took a chance, hired Van Eikeren, and brought him to San Francisco. "There is something I've wanted to do for a long time," he told Hans. "I want See's to be able to mass-produce truffles that taste better than the ones Godiva makes—and I want to be able to sell them at a better price."

At that time, Godiva had a corner on the truffle market in the United States. Godiva's clever advertising campaigns emphasized the company's European heritage and attempted to convince the American public that their chocolates were worth a premium price because of it. Yet in fact, Godiva U.S.A. is owned by the Campbell Soup Company, and the chocolates are manufactured in Redding, Pennsylvania, by its bakery division, Pepperidge Farms.

In January of 1982, Chuck Huggins turned Hans loose and assigned a team to work with him on truffle development. The first thing Hans did was sit down and call his friends in Holland, France, and Belgium. They sent him some 250 recipes for truffles.

"The next step," Hans said to Huggins, "is to try out these recipes and pick the best ones!" Months later, See's truffle-test team was waddling around, having taste-tested all the recipes, but they had a dozen winners.

Hans and his team then set out to identify a company to work with See's on developing custom production equipment for making the truffles. A Dutch engineering firm was chosen, and they spent six weeks at See's sketching prototypes, chalking out floor plans, and working out production details. The engineers went back to Holland, built the equipment, and returned to California to install it and get the production line up and running. On many days the team worked from 5 A.M. until midnight.

Finally, in August 1985, See's new line of truffles was ready for test marketing in two dozen shops in Seattle, Sacramento, and San Diego. Customer surveys revealed adjustments that needed to be made—the orange flavor was too strong, or the texture was not quite right. At last, by Christmas 1985, See's Truffles—a classic blend of fine dark, semi-sweet, or milk chocolate combined with dairy butter and heavy cream—were ready for prime time.

Mr. Huggins realized his dream of making high-quality truffles and offering them to the public at a better price than Godiva. Do See's taste better than Godiva truffles? Take a bite, and See for yourself.

A Chocolate Tie for Dad

These days most new ideas for recipes come from See's Research and Development Department, but sometimes concepts for new chocolate pieces come out of left field. Case in point: the Chocolate Father's Day Tie—an advertising idea that turned into a piece of chocolate.

It was the late 1980s and the award-winning Hal Riney Agency was handling advertising for See's Candies. Art Director Chris Chaffin had been assigned to create an ad for Father's Day. But he had a problem. See's didn't have a special Father's Day candy to offer that year. Undaunted, Chaffin

decided, "Why not pretend that See's R & D Department is working overtime to create something special for Dad, say, a Chocolate Tie. But, it won't be ready because they're still having trouble getting the tie-knot to look right. Everyone knows how hard it is to tie a Windsor knot—it's even more difficult with a *chocolate* tie."

The line read, "Our Chocolate Father's Day Tie Will Not Be Available This Year. How about a box of See's Peanut Brittle for Dad?"

Next, Chris had to come up with a "chocolate tie" for the photo shoot. He commissioned a movie-prop maker to carve a wooden tie to look like someone had taken a bite out of it. They added a Windsor knot, stripes, and See's logo—then covered the whole thing with shiny brown paint to make it look like glossy milk chocolate. Chaffin convinced See's Vice President of Marketing Dick Van Doren to pose for the ad.

The following year, someone had an idea. "Why not make a *real* chocolate tie for Father's Day?" They made a mold of the wooden tie used in the ad, and cast 50,000 Chocolate Ties from it. The Chocolate Ties sold out before Father's Day. See's sold Chocolate Ties for Father's Day for several years. Until someone thought of a Chocolate Hammer. And then Chocolate Seegars. And then . . .

OUR CHOCOLATE FATHER'S DAY TIE WILL NOT BE AVAILABLE THIS YEAR.

Our Vice President of Marketing—Mr. Dick Van Doren—says that
Research and Development is still having trouble with
the knots. But how about a box of See's Peanut Brittle for Dad?
Or See's Nuts and Chews? Or a miniature See's golf bag,
which holds five Lollypops, for only $3.00?

PART THREE

The Shops

Black and White and
Loved All Over

A Happy Habit

THE CANDY SHOPS CHARLES SEE FIRST OPENED IN LOS ANGELES all looked almost exactly the same: A white storefront with the black See's logo and lettering, a black-and-white awning over the shop window, and a slogan on the flair board out front like, "It's a Happy Habit."

Open the door of a See's shop and the first thing you'll see is the signature black-and-white tile floor polished to a high shine, sparkling white walls, and glass display cases filled with glossy chocolate confections. Here and there, curlicues of white wood trim and black detail can be seen. An old-fashioned writing desk with a fresh coat of white paint offers customers a pen with note cards to send to Aunt Martha along with a box of chocolates. A small white wastebasket sits next to the desk to catch botched cards. Art Deco light fixtures hang from the ceiling, looking like upside-down wedding cakes.

A portrait photograph of Mary See is displayed in its familiar cameo. Decorative touches like etched glass plates for the fudge and baby pictures on the walls complete the fanciful and homey look of a cottage kitchen, just like Mary See's at the turn of the 20th century.

In his day, Charles See worked to stay ahead of the competition in every aspect of the business, including his stores. Soda shops were the snazziest thing around in the 1920s, so he installed booths in some See's shops and sold finger sandwiches and malts. But in the long run, what people wanted was See's candy.

In the early '30s, Charles decided to try a brand-new look in See's shops—a play on the family name See and their love of the sea. Each shop window featured a miniature lighthouse with a blinking light on top. Some had a large sign out front in the shape of a lighthouse that lit up at night. But this new look didn't last long, and soon the country cottage look was back.

OPPOSITE: *The first See's shop in San Francisco on Polk Street, looks much the same today as when it opened in 1937—even its neighbor, Swan Oyster Depot, is the same.*

See's candy shop and ice-cream parlor, circa 1925.

74

All the World's a Fair

THE 1939 WORLD'S FAIR IN SAN FRANCISCO WAS A LANDMARK EVENT in the history of See's Candies.

By the end of the '30s, the company had been in operation for almost 20 years, and there were 49 See's Candies shops in 20 California cities. San Francisco was buzzing with activity in preparation for the grand opening of the Golden Gate International Exposition, to be held on Treasure Island. General Manager Ed Peck, who had a great feel for showmanship, decided that See's should have an exhibit at the Fair with a See's Candies shop and miniature candy kitchen where people could watch candy makers create Scotch Kisses and dip Bon Bons.

The See's Candies shop at the Exposition was a great success. Thousands of people from all over got their first taste of See's Candies there, and candy sales, at the going rate of 60 cents a pound, were phenomenal. Ed Peck recalled that "See's exhibit became one of the most popular attractions at the Fair, and really helped us take off."

See's CANDIES have gone to the FAIR
we cordially invite you to visit our EXHIBIT

Demonstrating the fine art of Bon Bon dipping in See's candy kitchen at the 1939 World's Fair.

MEET ME AT THE FAIR

The See's tradition, which began at the World's Fair in 1939, continued on with participation in state and county fairs, and at the 1982 World's Fair in Knoxville, Tennessee. In Knoxville, staff member Angelica Stoner, who has been with the company for more than 50 years, hired and trained young students from the nearby University of Tennessee in the art of bonbon and chocolate dipping for demonstrations in the See's shop at the Fair.

Crowds throng the See's exhibit on Treasure Island, a shop and candy kitchen built for the World's Fair.

Today, See's is present at community events throughout California and nearby states. See's restored 1930 Ford Model A roadsters and vintage Harley Davidson motorcycles with sidecars thrill parade-goers. Lollypops handed out along the parade route are part of the fun!

Rose Bowl Parades & The White Rabbit

L AURANCE SEE TOOK AN INNOVATIVE APPROACH TO SEE'S
advertising and public relations. Under his leadership, the company jumped
on the television bandwagon early, using the new medium to bring See's
Candies into living rooms nationwide. The tradition of watching the Rose Bowl
Parade on TV on New Year's Day and wondering what the See's float would look
like began in 1949.

Laurance proudly announced in a staff memo, "We were very happy indeed to
have See's represented in this year's Tournament of Roses Parade. . . . Our float was
included in several newsreels and its picture appeared in local newspapers and pic-
torial revues. It was also televised on New Year's Day."

For its first float in the Rose Bowl Parade, See's created a fifteen-foot-tall, snow-

white Easter Bunny pulling a cart with revolving Easter Egg wheels. Roses, carnations, sweet peas, and bachelor buttons were used in the design.

79

The giant floral Easter Bunny struck a deep chord with See's San Francisco manager, Ed Peck. Chuck Huggins recalls, "Ed Peck became so enamored of that rabbit that he begged Mr. See to allow him to have it in San Francisco. Mr. See agreed and shipped the giant rabbit north, where it was hoisted by crane on top of the See's building on Market Street. The fifteen-foot-tall rabbit was perched on the roof next to a motorized sign we called 'Waltzing Mary.' One side had a picture of Mary See, and the other a holiday greeting, and it rotated slowly around and around.

"Well, the mechanism on Waltzing Mary was a creaky chain drive that squeaked and squealed, and it drove the residents in nearby apartments crazy. When the chain drive jumped the track, it got unbearable, and on Saturday nights the neighbors would get worked up and start throwing their gin bottles at Peck's rabbit. It made a good target.

"One of my titles at the time was head of maintenance, and I would get late-night calls from Ed Peck to go fix the chain drive on Waltzing Mary so that the neighbors didn't destroy his rabbit with their bottles. This monster became known as the 'white rat' by those of us who had to protect it."

Dorothy Gray Forbes

Famous Old Time Candies

It's not unusual for people to find their life's work at See's Candies. Hundreds of employees have logged 25, 30, even 40 years or more of service. One 30-year-plus veteran of See's Candies, Director of Real Estate Mary Diamond, put it this way: "I feel like the people at See's are my family. I can't imagine being anywhere else."

Designer Dorothy Gray Forbes logged more than 50 years working for the company. In her long career at See's, Forbes created everything from shop posters and newspaper ads to See's signature candy box cover with its homey woodland cottage and cameo of Mary See. Untold millions of these box covers have been circulated worldwide, giving Dorothy's design arguably the widest distribution of any piece of graphic art in history.

Dorothy Gray Forbes's classic posters are still used in See's shops today.

OPPOSITE: *Dorothy Gray Forbes window-display card updated for 2005 by See's Graphic Design Manager Angela Fafara.*

An Easter Tradition

We Won't Be Winning Any Best-Dressed Awards

THE UNIFORM THAT SEE'S SALES CLERKS WEAR IS UNIQUE, TO say the least. Looking a bit like a traditional nurse's uniform with the addition of a jaunty black bow tie, it's a popular point of discussion among the women who wear it. When they are taking a lunch break, or stopping at the grocery store on the way home, the uniform inspires head-turning honks and waves from See's fans.

No matter what the era, visitors to See's shops are greeted with old-fashioned customer service by sales staff in crisp and classic attire. Though this kind of all-star service may no longer be in fashion elsewhere, at See's it never goes out of style.

OPPOSITE: *1930s "salesgirls" model See's original uniforms with black piping.*
RIGHT: *See's sales-staff uniforms in 1987 sport black bows.*

Mattel Barbie

See's "Barbie" is ready for business—from her white lace hairnet to her regulation uniform—though her hemline is a bit shorter than most See's sales staff. Posing in her own miniature See's shop, offering faux candy samples, this special limited-edition "Barbie" doll was introduced at the Berkshire Hathaway shareholders meeting in the spring of 2001. A blond, blue-eyed model dressed like the See's "Barbie" doll wowed the crowd when she presented the first doll to Chairman Warren Buffett and Vice Chairman Charles Munger. Shareholders placed orders for 10,000 dolls in advance sales on the spot. Now, See's "Barbie" is strictly a collector's item.

A Kid in a Candy Shop

THE COMFORTABLE FAMILIARITY OF SEE'S SHOPS IS ONLY PART of why you feel so good when you go into one of their stores. Greeted with a genuine smile as you approach the counter, before you can buy a thing, an amazing offer is made: "Would you like to try a sample?" If you hesitate for a moment, thinking it must be too good to be true, reassurance is quick to come. "Don't worry. It's free." No one knows exactly how or when this tradition began. One thing is certain: It will never change.

Today, See's shops are modern, efficient, and organized. You can grab your box of chocolates from the self-service section and dash on to your next errand, if you wish. See's even started taking those newfangled credit cards in, oh . . . the mid-1990s.

For many, a visit to See's is like dropping in on an old friend; it's a family tradition that brings back memories. Busy shoppers pause as one dad lifts up a wide-eyed toddler and carries her down the line of display cases, where dainty glass dishes lined with lace doilies hold candy samples. Ponytail bobbing, daughter and dad gaze at the chocolates, the peppermints, and the butterscotch lollypops. Grandparents point out long-time favorites, and a little girl discovers her first love.

Kids in a candy shop. Only some kids are 60. Some 30. And one has just turned 3. It's all part of the See's experience.

"Chocolate is a comfort food. Perhaps the reason that See's is so popular is that the stores themselves provide a comfort—a feeling of stepping into a gentler time. I savor every detail, inside and out . . . sort of like a fine See's chocolate truffle."

—Cherie Oliver, Redwood City, California

Laurance See proved to have the same visionary drive as his father. In the 1950s the population explosion in California resulted in tremendous suburban development. All those folks needed a place to shop, and the shopping mall was born. Early on, Laurance saw its potential and devised a plan to expand the company into shopping centers.

The first center See's moved into was the Town and Country Village in Sacramento. Then See's opened a shop in the Lakewood Mall near Long Beach. And on it went. By the end of the decade See's had expanded to 124 shops in California and 1,000 employees.

The '60s saw more growth for See's as the company expanded outside the state of California. Laurance anticipated that Phoenix would undergo the same population explosion as southern California. He was right. When an offer came from developer Del Webb to open a store in their mall in Phoenix, See's opened its first shop outside of California there. Seattle, Washington, came next. Then Portland, Oregon. Then Utah, followed by the first shop east of the Rockies in Denver, Colorado. By 1970 See's Candies was successfully established beyond the borders of California. And in California freestanding drive-in shops and more mall locations were planned and built.

By the late '80s, the familiar black and white See's logo began sprouting up on kiosks and carts in California airports. In January 2003, the first full-scale See's candy shop in an airport celebrated opening day at the San Francisco International Airport.

The opening of a new See's shop is a cause for celebration. From mariachis to New Orleans–style jazz bands, new See's shops always open to fanfare. These days there are far more new Holiday Gift Centers and airport kiosks opening up than full-scale See's shops, but in the 1970s and '80s, there was a new shop opening every other month. And every opening was an excuse to throw a party!

At the grand reopening of the See's shop at Kahala Mall in Honolulu, a group of local traditional Hawaiian musicians led by "Auntie Genoa" helped with the festivities. Famous in the islands, the group consists of three lively Hawaiian ladies in their 80s, who play ukuleles and sing traditional Hawaiian songs.

An enormous picture of Mary See with a wreath of flowers in her hair and a lei around her neck hangs in the entrance of the shop. Auntie Genoa took one look at the picture of Mary See and said, "You know, you can tell by looking at her that Mary See is one of us."

A Chinese Lion Dance and firecrackers marked the gala grand opening of the first See's Candies shop in the Ocean Ferry Terminal shopping plaza in Kowloon in 1976. Jim Trevor, a successful real estate developer and the former landlord of a See's shop in the Westlake Mall in northern California, took on the challenge of opening the first See's shop outside the United States in the golden years of his so-called retirement. He and his wife Jane were on a cruise with a stopover in Hong Kong when inspiration struck: Why not combine business and pleasure, living half the year in Asia and commuting home to the States for family weddings and the births of grandchildren? Chuck Huggins agreed that it was a grand idea and offered the assistance of retired sales manager Carol Henderson.

The Trevors and Carol were lucky to find two dynamic women in Hong Kong to co-manage the shop. Mary Jo Scott and Vivien Lee were friends and next-door neighbors who both happened to be married to professors at Hong Kong Polytechnic. Born in Shanghai, Vivien grew up in the States and is fluent in all the major Chinese dialects. She focused on marketing and now runs *four* See's Candies shops in Hong Kong. Mary Jo handled the business side of shop operations, and went on to become part of See's top management team in Cailfornia.

87

Asked about the challenges of doing business in Hong Kong, Jim Trevor remarked, "Anybody could sell See's Candies, even on the moon!"

The biggest and brassiest opening took place in January 1979 at #3 Embarcadero Center in San Francisco. It was a cold and blustery day, with a stiff wind coming off the Bay. The launch of the three-day event was scheduled for noon on a Thursday. The renowned Turk Murphy Jazz Band of Earthquake McGoon fame was booked to provide the music, and a tent was set up over the stage on a platform in front of the store.

See's high-energy PR man, Frank Rhylick, hired a platoon of fresh-faced young women to stand on street corners and hand out flyers to the downtown lunch crowd a week in advance. He also invited several busloads of elementary school children, re-cruited the newspapers, and sent invitations to all See's longtime business associates and suppliers. The opening was bound to be a success, but no one guessed just how big it would be.

At approximately 12:15 P.M. on opening day, crowds thronged the atrium in front of the shop. The chief of security for the Embar-cadero Center estimated that more than 10,000 people were milling around out front, listening to the music and trying to get into the shop for a free sample.

From then on, trombonist Turk Murphy and his band kept toes tapping at See's shop openings from the Pacific Coast to the Mississippi River. The band's popularity led to a weekly series of live radio broadcasts with vocalist Pat Yankee on KJAZ, sponsored by See's Candies. Directed by Bud Spangler, the radio series was broadcast live from See's shops in malls all over the Bay Area and from the elegant New Orleans Room at the Fairmont Hotel in San Francisco.

In January 1987, See's sponsored a Carnegie Hall Tribute to Turk Murphy in the last year of his life. Organized by bandleader Jim Cullum of The Jim Cullum Jazz Band, the event gave Chuck Huggins the opportunity to hear Cullum's Texas-based band perform for the first time. He was impressed with the band members' high level of musicianship, the excitement of their performances, and with Jim Cullum's depth of knowledge and feeling for the classics of jazz.

Two years later, Chuck received a call from Cullum. "Hey," Cullum shouted down the line from Texas, "I've got an idea! I'm thinking of starting a live radio show from our club in San Antonio and thought of you." It was the beginning of a long association between See's Candies and Jim Cullum's *Riverwalk Jazz* series, broadcast weekly on public radio stations nationwide for over 15 years. To this day, See's continues to support the radio series that originates from The Landing in San Antonio on PRI, Public Radio International.

See's love and support of jazz does not stop there. See's Candies supports jazz education projects like the Stanford Jazz Workshop and jazz festivals throughout the West.

89

RIGHT: *Turk Murphy*

Power to the People: See's the Day!

The Story of Shop 26

SOMETIMES THE MANAGEMENT AT SEE'S IS FACED WITH THE tough decision to close a shop. Just such an occasion arose in Oakland, California, in the spring of 2004. See's Shop 26 at 3295 Lakeshore Avenue had been operating in the red for quite some time.

Mulling over the decision to close Shop 26 was particularly difficult because the shop had been in operation since 1938, one of a handful of "historic" See's shops with the original Art Deco light fixtures and displays from the '30s. Finally, the decision was made. The losses were too great. Shop 26 would close on May 12, 2004.

The rumor got out. Hundreds of touching letters came in from families who had been visiting the store for generations.

As word spread, thousands of people signed petitions. The turning point came one evening at a fancy dress affair for the Art Deco Society of the San Francisco Bay area. As Chuck Huggins and his wife Donna entered the room, Laurie Gordon and two other members of the Art Deco Society, self-appointed guardians of See's Lakeshore Store, got down on their knees and begged him to keep the store open. Their entreaty was the final plea that made him rescind his decision.

The announcement was made to the press. Shop 26 would stay open.

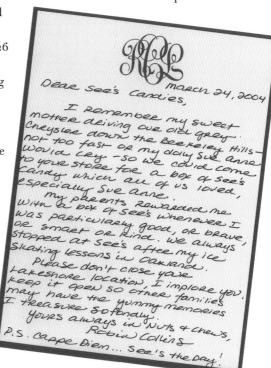

Dear See's Candies,   March 24, 2004

I remember my sweet mother driving our old grey Chrysler down the Berkeley Hills — not too fast or my dolly Sue Anne would cry — so we could come to your store for a box of See's candy which all of us loved, especially Sue Anne.

My parents rewarded me with a box of See's whenever I was particularly good, or brave, or smart or kind. We always stopped at See's after my ice skating lessons in Oakland.

Please don't close your Lakeshore location, I implore you. Keep it open so other families may have the yummy memories I treasure so fondly.

Yours always in Nuts & Chews,
Robin Collins

P.S. Carpe Diem... See's the Day!

Lucy Loves See's

One day in 1952 the phone rang in Plant Manager Forrest Jordan's office at the See's facility on La Cienega in Los Angeles. A producer from the *I Love Lucy Show* was on the line. "We want to do an episode with Lucy and Ethel on the production line in a candy company. Will you help us?"

The answer, of course, was, "Yes—why don't you come on over and we'll show you around." Lucille Ball and Vivian Vance spent half a day learning the ropes, dipping chocolates, and packing candy on the production line at See's.

Titled "Job Switching," the show was first broadcast on September 15, 1952 and became one of the all-time most popular episodes of *I Love Lucy*. The usual comic plot twists land Lucy and Ethel with jobs in a candy factory. Frantically trying to keep up with the production line, they wind up stuffing chocolates into their pockets and bras—and into their mouths.

Even though the See's name was never used in the episode, *I Love Lucy* and See's Candies are forever linked in the public imagination due, in part, to a network TV news feature that has been rebroadcast several times. As the TV crew was about to film the packing line, the producer talked Chuck Huggins into trying his hand at packing two-pound boxes of See's Candies on the line. Here's how he tells it:

"They put me in the middle on the conveyor belt line. And I couldn't keep up. The women working with me were all giving me the raspberry. I could see the camera coming close. I could hear the hostess of the TV show saying, 'And here's the president of See's Candies. As you can see, this is no easy task—as he is demonstrating.' And they cut, back and forth, between me trying to keep up with the conveyor belt and the famous TV episode with Lucy and Ethel."

Going the Extra Mile

IT SEEMS THAT ALMOST EVERYONE WHO GREW UP IN CALIFORNIA in the past century remembers See's Candies as being a part of their family traditions. When they think back on those times, they remember See's.

"Each time I enter a See's store, I'm reminded of the See's trips I used to take with my grandmother, where she would choose a dark chocolate marzipan and I would choose a dark chocolate raspberry cream. I have taken comfort in the consistency of See's candy stores. They have always been there as a link to the past."

—Moya Stone, Moraga, California

See's customers are passionate about one thing: They don't want See's Candies to change, not even the frosting decoration on its Easter Eggs. So, whether it's finding the very last Fourth of July "Firecracker" for a frantic parent, or hiding a diamond ring in a traditional red velvet heart, Assistant Customer Service Director Johnnie Woods and all See's employees hold that trust sacred.

Customer Service and Community Service go hand-in-hand at See's Candies. When the Northridge earthquake struck the Los Angeles area in 1991, See's distributed 40,000 pounds of candy to the people living in temporary shelters. See's also makes substantial donations to nonprofit organizations supporting health services, education, the arts, and groups serving young people, such as Tenaya Elementary School, Berkeley High School Jazz Ensemble, Carson High School, the Boys and Girls Clubs, Culver City High School, the Family Service Agency, South San Francisco High School, the Music in Schools Today program, and more.

"Every Easter my brothers and I would each receive a huge See's Chocolate Fudge Easter Egg (with nuts). We would savor each morsel, trying to make ours last the longest. Whoever finished first was out of luck, because although we shared everything else, our chocolate egg from See's was another story."

—Ann Schramer, Mission Viejo, California

A Century of Candy Making

OPPOSITE: *Laurance See opened the first shop in the Stanford Shopping Center in 1957. After relocating to larger premises in the center in 2005, the shop still displays many of the same distinctive features—the striped awning and the black and white motif—as the original See's shops in the 1920s.*

IN 1921, THE EQUITY OF SEE'S CANDIES AMOUNTED TO ONE STORE in Los Angeles and the dream of a young man who had a strong desire to make something of himself. Today, See's Candies has 200 shops and close to 100 Holiday Gift Centers. Forty licensees operate See's kiosks in airports, stores, and See's overseas locations. The company employs up to 6,000 people at its busiest time of year, fulfills some 450,000 mail orders annually, and receives more than 2 million visitors worldwide at its Web site each year!

Looking back over almost a century of candy making, at the heart of the See's story is Charles See's belief in quality and his faith in the simple concept of building a business based on quality and integrity. And looking to the future, a source of great security and comfort is the continued benefit from the Berkshire Hathaway ownership, and the leadership of Warren Buffet and Charlie Munger, two men who share the same ethics as the See family.

95

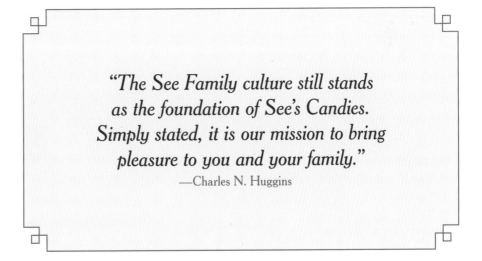

"The See Family culture still stands as the foundation of See's Candies. Simply stated, it is our mission to bring pleasure to you and your family."
—Charles N. Huggins

ACKNOWLEDGMENTS

I am grateful to Chuck Huggins and to See's Candies for the wonderful opportunity to delve into the history of the company and tell its fascinating story. I appreciate the countless hours that Chuck has spent instilling in me the history that he inherited and that he has lived for the past half century. However, any inaccuracies or deficiencies in the text are wholly my own.

I was first introduced to the idea of writing a book about See's Candies in a hurried backstage conversation with Donna Huggins at a jazz concert in July 2003. Donna's passion and commitment propelled the idea into action, and her counsel has been an important part of the process every step of the way.

Angela Fafara, See's Graphic Design Manager, deserves special credit for her deep involvement in the book. Together, Angela and I sifted through crates and boxes of old letters, photographs, business records, advertising layouts, and packaging designs. On many occasions, Angela helped talk me through the concept of the book, decided which graphic pieces best told the story, and did the hands-on sleuthing to find answers to the esoteric details of candy making. Angela's fine abilities as a designer can be seen and felt in this book.

The sifting and sorting of See's artifacts and memorabilia continued at my office, where Melody Sober wrangled banker's boxes full of photographs and documents into manageable files and folders.

I am grateful to Kevin Toyama, Project Coordinator at Chronicle Books, who helped us focus the story and brought his considerable experience and thoughtful guidance to the project.

Special thanks are also due to the following See's Candies staff members: Nancy Bernard, Executive Assistant to the President; Maggie Garrison, Purchasing Manager, Raw Materials; Carol Gregor, Director of HGC and Licensees; Karen Gard, Director of Purchasing and Procurement; Eileen Duag, Director of Product Support; Steve Ferrando, Director of Product Development; Jim Tremont, Corporate Secretary; and Dick Van Doren, Vice President of Marketing, who generously gave their time to the project.

It has been my great pleasure to become acquainted with all the talented and dedicated staff at See's Candies.

—*Margaret Moos Pick*

Milk Chocolate Butter
Chocolate buttercream

Dark Chocolate Butter
Chocolate buttercream

Milk Buttercream
Vanilla buttercream

Milk Bordeaux
*Brown sugar
buttercream*

Dark Bordeaux
Brown sugar buttercream

Pecan Buds
Pecans and vanilla caramel

Milk Waln
English waln

Milk Peanuts
Roasted peanuts

Raspberry Truffle
Rich raspberry chocolate

Almond Buds
Roasted almonds and caramel

California Brittle
*Hard toffee
with almonds*

Butterchew
*Vanilla brown sugar
caramel with dark
chocolate coating*

Dark Chocolate Chip Truffle
*Rich chocolate buttercream
with chocolate chips*

Maple Waln
Maple buttercrea
English waln

Cocoanut
Coconut buttercream

Polar Bear Paws
Peanuts and vanilla caramel

Lemon Truffle
*Rich lemon chiffon
buttercream*

Orange Cream
Orange buttercream

Strawberry Cream
*Strawberry buttercream
with strawberries*

Raspberry Cream
*Raspberry buttercream
with raspberries*

Vanilla Nut Cr
Vanilla buttercrea
English waln

Walnut Square
Caramel with English walnuts

Almond Square
Roasted almonds and caramel

Peanut Nougat
Chewy peanut nougat